EMMA S. CLARK MEMORIAL LIBRARY
Setauket, L.I., New York 11733

No One Is the Same

Appreciating Differences

BY ALYSSA KREKELBERG

Published by The Child's World®
1980 Lookout Drive • Mankato, MN 56003-1705
800-599-READ • www.childsworld.com

Photographs ©: Shutterstock Images, cover, 1, 10, 13, 14; Wave Break Media/iStockphoto, 5, 6, 9; iStockphoto, 17, 18, 21

Copyright © 2021 by The Child's World®
All rights reserved. No part of this book may be reproduced or utilized in any form or by any means without written permission from the publisher.

ISBN 9781503844568 (Reinforced Library Binding)
ISBN 9781503846692 (Portable Document Format)
ISBN 9781503847880 (Online Multi-user eBook)
LCCN 2019956597

Printed in the United States of America

Alyssa Krekelberg is a children's book editor and author. She lives in Minnesota with her hyper husky.

Contents

CHAPTER ONE
When Someone Needs Help . . . 4

CHAPTER TWO
Learning from Each Other . . . 11

CHAPTER THREE
Asking Questions . . . 16

Glossary . . . 22
To Learn More . . . 23
Index . . . 24

CHAPTER ONE

When Someone Needs Help

Katie uses a wheelchair to help her get around. It makes many things easier for Katie. But some things are still hard.

Jenna notices that Katie cannot reach the top bookshelf. Jenna thinks about how she would feel if she could not reach something. She would feel **frustrated**.

It is important to know that some people face different struggles than others.

"Can I help you get a book?" Jenna asks.

"Yes, thank you," Katie says. "I **appreciate** that you asked me first."

Jenna smiles. "Just like you asked me this morning if I needed help with my spelling homework."

Jenna and Katie have many differences. Katie uses a wheelchair. Jenna needs help with her spelling homework. However, the two friends are always there to help one another.

Differences can make a friendship stronger.

Some people might need extra help reading if English is not their first language.

CHAPTER TWO

Learning from Each Other

Adam moved to the United States from France. He and Michael are in the same reading group.

Adam can speak English, but he has trouble reading it. Adam does not read along with the teacher. Instead, Adam looks away.

Michael thinks about how he would feel if he moved to a different country. He might not know the language. He might feel bad if he could not read the things around him, such as books.

That day at recess, Michael asks Adam questions about France. He also asks if Adam would like help in their reading group.

It can be helpful to think about how someone else may feel.

Working together can be good for everyone.

The two boys help each other. Michael learns a lot about a different country. And Adam gets better at reading English. They learn a lot from each other because they have different backgrounds.

When is a time you helped someone who was different from you? How did it make you feel?

How are you and your friends different? How are you the same?

CHAPTER THREE

Asking Questions

Benjamin's friend Amara wears a **hijab** every day. It covers her hair and neck. She is the only one in Benjamin's class who wears a hijab.

Hijabs can come in many different colors.

Asking respectful questions is a good way to learn about other people.

Benjamin is **curious** about Amara's hijab. No one in his family wears clothing like it. He asks Amara why she wears her hijab.

Amara says that she wears a hijab because of her **religion**. Her mom and sisters all wear them, too.

"My mom wears a necklace shaped like a cross," Benjamin says. "She wears that because of her religion, too."

Benjamin did not know that people from other religions might wear different types of clothing. He is glad to have learned more about his friend.

It is important to appreciate your friends' differences.

GLOSSARY

appreciate (uh-PREE-shee-ayt) To appreciate something is to like it. A friend might appreciate it if you ask if he or she needs help.

curious (KYUR-ee-uhs) Someone who is curious is interested in learning about something. Benjamin was curious about his friend Amara's hijab.

frustrated (FRUS-tray-ted) Someone who is frustrated is upset about not being able to do something. Katie was frustrated in the library.

hijab (hi-JAHB) A hijab is a religious covering for someone's neck and hair. Amara wore her hijab every day.

religion (ri-LIJ-uhn) Religion is a certain system of belief and worship. Some people wear hijabs because of their religion.

Books

Merk, T. M. *Painting a Peaceful Picture: Respecting Peers*. Mankato, MN: The Child's World, 2019.

Penfold, Alexandra. *All Are Welcome*. New York, NY: Alfred A. Knopf, 2018.

Richards, Doyin. *What's the Difference?* New York, NY: Feiwel and Friends, 2017.

Websites

Visit our website for links about appreciating differences:
childsworld.com/links

Note to Parents, Teachers, and Librarians: We routinely verify our Web links to make sure they are safe and active sites. So encourage your readers to check them out!

INDEX

appreciation, 7

English, 11, 15

France, 11, 12
frustration, 4

helping, 7–8, 12, 15
hijabs, 16–19

reading, 11–15
recess, 12
religions, 19–20

United States, 11

wheelchairs, 4–8